Teaching Kids About Money

Smart Money Moves for Kids

By Eamon Lawler

Foreword

In "Teaching Kids About Money: Smart Money Moves for Kids," Eamon Lawler delivers a valuable resource for parents, educators, and anyone passionate about equipping the next generation with essential financial skills. With a blend of expertise and a genuine understanding of the challenges children face in today's complex financial landscape, Lawler offers practical insights and actionable strategies. This book is not just a guide; it's a roadmap to empower young minds with the knowledge and habits they need to navigate the world of money responsibly.

As we embark on this journey with Lawler, let us embrace the importance of shaping a financially literate future—one where our children are equipped to make smart money moves from an early age.

Table of Contents

CHAPTER 1

Introduction to Money

- **Why Teach Kids About Money?**

Teaching kids about money is a fundamental aspect of their education that extends far beyond the mere exchange of currency. The importance of financial education for children cannot be overstated, as it lays the groundwork for responsible financial behaviors, fosters a sense of economic awareness, and equips them with essential life skills.

1. Foundational Life Skills:

Introducing financial concepts at an early age helps children develop foundational life skills. Budgeting, saving, and understanding the value of money are essential aspects of personal finance that contribute to a child's overall development. These skills not only impact their financial well-being but also shape their ability to plan, set goals, and make informed decisions throughout their lives.

2. Responsible Spending Habits:
   Teaching kids about money instills the concept of responsible spending. By understanding that money is a finite resource, children learn to

prioritize their needs and wants. This early exposure to responsible financial behavior lays the groundwork for making thoughtful spending choices in adulthood, preventing impulsive and unsustainable financial decisions.

3. Financial Independence:
Financial literacy empowers children to become financially independent adults. As they grasp the concepts of earning, saving, and

investing, they gain the confidence to navigate the complexities of the financial world. This knowledge sets the stage for a future where they can manage their finances, plan for major life events, and build a secure financial foundation.

4. Work Ethic and Goal Setting:
   Learning about money often involves understanding the connection between work and earnings. This connection cultivates

a strong work ethic as children realize the effort required to earn money. Additionally, financial education encourages goal setting, whether it's saving for a toy, a bike, or future education. This early exposure to goal setting becomes a transferable skill applicable to various aspects of life.

5. Critical Thinking and Problem-Solving:

Financial education stimulates critical thinking and problem-solving skills. Children encounter real-world scenarios that require them to analyze options, make decisions, and consider consequences. Whether it's deciding how to allocate their allowance or weighing the pros and cons of a purchase, these experiences contribute to the development of sound decision-making skills.

6. Preventing Debt and Financial Strain:

Understanding the implications of debt and the importance of living within one's means is crucial for avoiding financial strain in adulthood. Kids who learn about money early are more likely to develop a cautious approach to borrowing and spending, reducing the risk of falling into debt traps later in life.

7. Building Generational Wealth:

Financial education lays the foundation for building generational wealth. When children learn to manage money wisely, save, and invest, they contribute to a legacy of financial stability that can extend beyond their own lives. This knowledge becomes a powerful tool for breaking cycles of financial insecurity and creating opportunities for future generations.

In conclusion, teaching kids about money is an investment in their future well-being. The skills and habits acquired through financial education pave the way for responsible and empowered individuals who can navigate the complexities of the modern financial landscape with confidence and competence.

- **The Importance of Financial Literacy**

Financial literacy for kids is of paramount importance, shaping their understanding of money and laying the groundwork for a financially responsible and secure future. Here are key reasons why fostering financial literacy in children is crucial:

1. Early Habit Formation:

Introducing financial concepts at a young age helps in the formation of positive financial habits. Children learn the value of saving, budgeting, and responsible spending early on, setting the stage for a lifetime of sound financial practices.

2. Empowerment and Confidence: Financial literacy empowers children to navigate the financial world with confidence. Understanding basic financial

principles gives them a sense of

control over their economic future

and fosters the confidence to make

informed financial decisions.

3. Prevention of Financial Mistakes:

   A lack of financial literacy can

lead to costly mistakes in adulthood.

Teaching kids about money helps

prevent common pitfalls such as

excessive debt, impulsive spending,

and financial mismanagement by

instilling a sense of financial responsibility and prudence.

4. Introduction to Earning and Work Ethic:

Financial education often involves teaching kids about the concept of earning. This connection between work and money encourages the development of a strong work ethic, instilling the idea that financial success is often tied to effort and diligence.

5. Critical Thinking and Decision-Making Skills:

Financial literacy promotes critical thinking and decision-making skills. Children learn to analyze choices, consider consequences, and make thoughtful financial decisions. These skills extend beyond money matters, benefiting various aspects of their lives.

6. Understanding the Value of Money:

Financial literacy helps children understand the value of money and appreciate the effort required to earn it. This awareness fosters a sense of gratitude and a more mindful approach to spending, reducing the likelihood of entitlement or wasteful habits.

7. Preparation for Life Transitions:

As children grow, they will face significant life transitions that involve financial decisions—such as going to college, buying a car, or renting an apartment. Financial literacy equips them with the knowledge and skills needed to navigate these transitions successfully.

8. Building Savings and Investments:
Financial education introduces the concepts of saving and investing.

Kids who grasp these principles early are more likely to develop a habit of saving money for future goals and understand the potential benefits of long-term investments.

9. Crisis Preparedness:
   Financial literacy prepares children for unexpected financial challenges. Understanding the importance of an emergency fund and having basic financial planning skills can make them more resilient

in the face of economic
uncertainties.

10. Setting the Stage for Future
Generations:

Teaching kids about money not
only benefits them individually but
also contributes to building a
financially literate society. Children
who grow up with a strong
foundation in financial literacy are
more likely to pass on these skills to

future generations, breaking cycles of financial instability.

In essence, instilling financial literacy in children is an investment in their well-being, empowering them to make informed choices and navigate the complexities of personal finance with competence and confidence throughout their lives.

CHAPTER 2

Money Basics Made Fun

- **Counting and Managing Money**

Making counting and managing money easy for kids involves incorporating interactive and engaging activities that simplify financial concepts. Here are some effective strategies:

1. Use Real Money:

   Provide children with real coins and bills to handle. The tangible experience of touching and counting actual currency helps them understand the physical representation of value.

2. Play Money Games:

   Turn learning into a game. Use board games or online games that involve transactions and counting money. Games like Monopoly or online simulations can make the process enjoyable and educational.

3. Create a Pretend Store:

   Set up a pretend store at home where children can "buy" and "sell" items using play money. This hands-on activity introduces them to the concept of making purchases and receiving change.

4. Use Visual Aids:

Utilize visual aids like charts, graphs, or illustrations to represent different denominations and their values. Visualizing the concept of money can enhance understanding, especially for younger children.

5. Teach Basic Math Skills:

Reinforce basic math skills related to money, such as addition and subtraction. Start with simple examples, like adding coins of the same denomination, and gradually

progress to more complex
calculations.

6. Create a Savings Jar:

   Introduce the idea of saving by
setting up a savings jar. Encourage
children to deposit a portion of
their allowance or money gifts into
the jar regularly. This helps them
see the accumulation of savings over
time.

7. Allowance System:

Implement an allowance system where children receive a set amount of money on a regular basis. This provides practical experience in budgeting and decision-making as they allocate funds for spending, saving, and, if applicable, giving.

8. Set Financial Goals:

Help kids establish simple financial goals, such as saving for a toy or a special treat. This introduces the concept of setting objectives and working towards them through budgeting and saving.

9. Storytelling:

Use relatable stories or scenarios to explain financial concepts. Create fictional characters who encounter financial situations, allowing children to connect with the concepts on a personal level.

10. Involve Them in Shopping:

Bring children along when shopping and involve them in the decision-making process. Compare prices, discuss budgeting considerations, and let them make small choices to reinforce the value of money.

11. Online Educational Resources:
Explore age-appropriate online resources designed to teach kids about money. Many websites and apps offer interactive games and

lessons that make learning about

finances entertaining.

12. Model Good Financial Behavior:

   Children learn by observing.

Model good financial behavior by

discussing your own spending

decisions, budgeting, and saving

practices. This provides real-world

examples for them to emulate.

   By incorporating these strategies,

you can make counting and managing

money a fun and practical learning experience for kids, setting the foundation for their financial literacy and responsibility.

- **Budgeting in a Kid-Friendly Way**

Teaching kids about budgeting in a kid-friendly way involves simplifying the concept and making it relatable.

Here's a step-by-step guide to make budgeting easy and engaging for children:

1. Introduce the Concept:
   Start by explaining that a budget is like a plan for their money. Use simple language and relate it to something they understand, like planning for a special event or deciding how many toys they can buy.

2. Identify Income:

Help children understand where their money comes from. This could include their allowance, money received as gifts, or any other sources. Emphasize the importance of knowing how much money they have to work with.

3. Categorize Expenses:

Break down spending into basic categories that are relevant to kids, such as toys, snacks, and activities.

This simplifies the budgeting process and makes it more relatable.

4. Set Goals:

Encourage goal-setting by discussing what they want to save for or buy. Whether it's a new toy or a special treat, having specific goals motivates kids to allocate their money wisely.

5. Create a Visual Budget:

Use visuals like charts or drawings to represent income and expenses. This could be a simple pie chart or a drawing of jars labeled with different spending categories. Visual aids make the budgeting process more tangible.

6. Allocate Funds:

Help children divide their money into categories based on their goals and needs. For example, if they want a new toy, allocate a portion of their money towards the "Toy Fund." This teaches them to prioritize and allocate resources.

8. Decision-Making Scenarios:
   Present simple scenarios that require decision-making. For instance, if they want to buy a snack and a small toy but have limited money, discuss the trade-offs and help them make choices based on their budget.

9. Adjust and Reflect:

Regularly review and adjust the budget based on changing goals or circumstances. This reinforces the idea that budgets are flexible and can be adapted as needed.

10. Celebrate Achievements:

Celebrate when they reach their savings goals. Positive reinforcement reinforces good budgeting habits and makes the process more enjoyable.

11. Involve Them in Family Budgeting:

If appropriate, involve kids in discussions about family expenses. This can provide a broader understanding of budgeting and financial responsibility within the context of a household.

12. Use Technology:

Explore kid-friendly budgeting apps or online tools that make the process interactive. Some apps are designed specifically for children and provide a visually appealing way to manage money.

By making budgeting relatable, visual, and goal-oriented, you can simplify the concept for kids and instill valuable financial skills that will benefit them as they grow older.

CHAPTER 3

Earning and Saving

- **Teaching Kids to Earn Money Responsibly**

Teaching kids to earn money responsibly involves instilling a strong work ethic, financial responsibility, and an understanding of the value of money. Here's a guide to help parents and educators in this process:

1. Chores and Responsibilities:
   Connect the idea of earning money with completing tasks around the house. Assign age-appropriate chores and responsibilities, emphasizing that money is earned through effort and contribution.

2. Discuss the Concept of Earning:

Explain that money is a reward for work. Engage in age-appropriate conversations about why people work, linking it to meeting needs, achieving goals, and contributing to the family or community.

3. Encourage Entrepreneurial Ventures:

Support entrepreneurial activities by helping kids identify their interests and talents. Whether it's a small business like a lemonade stand or providing a service like pet sitting, these ventures teach valuable lessons about initiative and financial reward.

4. Set Clear Expectations:
   Clearly communicate the expectations for earning money. Discuss the type and frequency of tasks required to receive payment. This clarity helps children understand the connection between effort and compensation.

5. Introduce Savings and Spending:

Teach kids the importance of allocating earned money wisely. Encourage them to set aside a portion for savings and budget for spending. This instills early lessons in budgeting and delayed gratification.

6. Use a Reward System:

Implement a reward system for completed tasks. This could involve a small allowance or a system where they earn points toward a specific reward. Reinforce the idea that responsibility and effort are directly linked to financial gain.

7. Discuss Money Values:

Incorporate discussions about values related to money. Teach kids about the importance of sharing, giving to others, and making thoughtful spending choices. Instilling these values early contributes to responsible financial behavior.

8. Open a Bank Account:

Consider opening a savings account for your child. This introduces the concept of banking, interest, and saving for the future. Many banks offer accounts specifically designed for children.

9. Teach Negotiation and Communication Skills:

If applicable, involve kids in negotiations for their services. This could be discussing payment for additional chores or negotiating prices for a small business. These experiences develop valuable communication and negotiation skills.

10. Lead by Example:

Model responsible financial behavior. Share your own experiences with earning, saving, and spending. Children often learn by observing, so demonstrating responsible money management sets a powerful example.

11. Discuss Work Goals:

Engage in conversations about their work goals. Ask them what they want to achieve with their earnings, whether it's saving for a specific item, donating to a cause, or investing in their education. This encourages goal-setting and planning.

12. Address Mistakes Positively:

If they make financial mistakes, use them as learning opportunities. Discuss what went wrong, why, and how they can make better choices in the future. Encourage resilience and a positive approach to learning from experiences.

By incorporating these strategies, parents and educators can guide children toward earning money responsibly, imparting valuable skills that will serve them well in their financial journeys.

- **Teaching About Savings**

Teaching kids about the value of saving is a crucial lesson that sets the foundation for a lifetime of financial responsibility. Here are

strategies to convey the importance
of saving to children:

1. Start Early:

Introduce the concept of saving
money from a young age. The earlier
children learn about saving, the
more ingrained the habit becomes.

2. Set Savings Goals:

Help kids set specific savings
goals. Whether it's for a toy, a
game, or a special treat, having

tangible objectives makes the
concept of saving more concrete and
motivating.

3. Use a Savings Jar or Piggy Bank:
   Provide a visual representation of
saving by using a jar or piggy bank.
Kids can physically see their money
accumulating, reinforcing the idea
that saving leads to tangible results.

4. Allocate Allowance to Savings:

If your child receives an allowance, encourage them to allocate a portion of it to savings. This practice instills the habit of saving a consistent percentage of their income.

5. Teach Delayed Gratification:

Emphasize the concept of delayed gratification. Discuss how waiting and saving for something special can be more satisfying than instant but fleeting purchases.

6. Explain Interest:

   Introduce the concept of interest in a simple way. Explain that some savings accounts grow over time, earning a little extra money, which can serve as a reward for saving.

7. Celebrate Savings Milestones:

   Celebrate when they reach certain savings milestones. This positive reinforcement reinforces the idea that saving is an achievement worth recognizing.

8. Involve Them in Purchase Decisions:

When making family purchases, involve children in the decision-making process. Discuss whether to spend saved money on a shared family item or continue saving for individual goals.

9. Teach Comparison Shopping:

Teach kids the value of shopping around for the best prices. This can be a valuable lesson in stretching their saved money further and making informed spending choices.

10. Share Personal Stories:

Share personal stories about the benefits of saving. Talk about instances where saving money helped you achieve a goal or navigate unexpected expenses. Personal

anecdotes can make the concept
more relatable.

11. Introduce Long-Term Savings:
   Discuss the idea of saving for the
future. This could involve setting
aside money for bigger goals like
education, a special trip, or even
long-term savings for adulthood.

12. Be Consistent and Patient:
   Building a saving habit takes time.
Be consistent in encouraging saving,

and be patient as children develop

this important financial skill.

By incorporating these strategies,

parents and educators can

effectively convey the value of

saving to children, laying the

groundwork for a financially

responsible and secure future.

CHAPTER 4

Spending Wisely

- **Differentiating Between Needs and Wants**

Teaching kids to differentiate between needs and wants is a crucial aspect of financial education. Here are strategies to help children understand the distinction between these two concepts:

1. Define Basic Needs:

Start by explaining the concept of basic needs, such as food, shelter, clothing, and healthcare. Emphasize that these are essential for survival and well-being.

2. Discuss Wants:

Introduce wants as things that are desirable but not necessary for survival. Use relatable examples like toys, video games, or sweets to illustrate the difference between needs and wants.

3. Interactive Sorting Activity:

Engage kids in a hands-on activity where they sort pictures or objects into categories of needs and wants. This visual exercise helps reinforce the distinction in a tangible way.

4. Role-Playing Scenarios:

Create hypothetical scenarios and ask kids to identify whether the item or activity in question is a need or a want. This encourages critical thinking and application of the concept.

5. Relate to Personal Experiences:
Encourage children to think about their own lives. Ask them to identify things they need for school versus things they want. Relating the

concept to their own experiences
makes it more relevant.

6. Use Storytelling:

   Tell stories or read books that
highlight characters making
decisions between needs and wants.
This narrative approach can make
the concept more engaging and
memorable.

7. Budgeting Games:

Play budgeting games that involve allocating limited resources between needs and wants. This interactive approach helps children understand the trade-offs involved in decision-making.

8. Create a "Needs vs. Wants" List: Collaboratively create a list of needs and wants. Discuss and review the list regularly, reinforcing the understanding of these categories.

9. Discuss Advertising Influence:

Talk about how advertisements often try to convince people that wants are actually needs. Discussing advertising influence helps children become more discerning consumers.

10. Encourage Prioritization:

Teach kids to prioritize their spending by distinguishing between more urgent needs and less immediate wants. This skill is valuable for budgeting and decision-making.

11. Set Spending Limits:

When giving kids allowances, set spending limits for needs and wants. This practical experience helps them make choices within defined financial boundaries.

12. Ask Open-Ended Questions:

Encourage critical thinking by asking open-ended questions about needs and wants. For example, "Why do you think having a bed is a need?" This prompts thoughtful consideration.

13. Lead by Example:

Demonstrate the differentiation between needs and wants through your own behavior. Discuss your own decision-making process when it comes to spending on essentials versus non-essential items.

Consistency and repetition are key when teaching this concept. By employing these strategies, parents and educators can help children develop a fundamental understanding of distinguishing between needs and wants, fostering responsible decision-making in their financial choices.

- **Making Smart Purchase Decisions**

Teaching kids to make smart purchase decisions is a valuable skill that contributes to their financial literacy. Here are strategies to impart this skill effectively:

1. Discuss Decision-Making Factors: Teach kids to consider various factors when making a purchase, such as price, quality, and utility.

Discuss how these factors influence their choices.

2. Set a Budget:

Introduce the concept of budgeting. Encourage children to allocate their money wisely by setting spending limits for different categories. This helps instill responsible financial habits.

3. Compare Prices:

Teach kids to compare prices before making a purchase. This can be a simple activity while shopping together, whether online or at a store. Discussing the value of finding the best deal reinforces the concept of smart spending.

4. Prioritize Needs and Wants:

Reinforce the difference between needs and wants. Encourage kids to prioritize their purchases based on

necessity and importance, fostering
a mindful approach to spending.

5. Quality Over Quantity:
   Emphasize the importance of
quality over quantity. Teach kids
that sometimes spending a bit more
on a higher-quality item can be a
smarter long-term decision.

6. Consider Long-Term Value:
   Discuss the long-term value of a
purchase. Help kids understand that

some items may cost more initially but provide greater value over time, emphasizing the concept of investments.

7. Avoid Impulse Purchases:

Teach the importance of resisting impulse purchases. Encourage kids to take time to think about whether they truly need or want an item, reducing impulsive buying behavior.

8. Introduce the 24-Hour Rule:

Suggest implementing the 24-hour rule for significant purchases. Encourage kids to wait a day before making a decision, giving them time to reflect on whether the purchase is necessary.

9. Teach Consumer Rights:

Educate children about their rights as consumers. Discuss the importance of fair treatment, understanding product warranties,

and the ability to return or
exchange items.

10. Discuss Advertising Tactics:

Help kids become critical
consumers by discussing common
advertising tactics. Explain how
advertisements often emphasize the
positive aspects of a product and
how to look beyond marketing
messages.

11. Practice Decision-Making

Scenarios:

Role-play different purchase

scenarios with kids. Present them

with choices and discuss the pros

and cons of each option, helping

them develop decision-making skills.

12. Encourage Saving for Goals:

Connect smart purchase decisions

with savings goals. Teach kids that

making thoughtful choices with their

money can lead to achieving larger financial objectives.

14. Reflect on Past Decisions:

Encourage kids to reflect on past purchase decisions. Discuss what worked well and what they might do differently next time. This reflection promotes continuous improvement in decision-making skills.

By incorporating these strategies, parents and educators can guide children toward making smart purchase decisions, equipping them with essential skills for financial responsibility.

CHAPTER 5

Investing Basics

- **Simple Concepts of Investing**

Teaching kids about investing can be approached with simple concepts to lay the foundation for understanding. Here are some straightforward ideas to introduce the concept of investing to children:

1. Explaining Ownership:

   Describe investing as a way to become an owner of a small piece of a company. Relate it to owning a share of a favorite toy or game, helping them understand the idea of ownership in a business.

2. Discussing Growth:

   Emphasize the concept of growth over time. Explain that when they invest money, it has the potential to grow, just like plants or trees. This introduces the basic idea of compounding and the benefits of patience.

3. Using Real-world Examples:

Share simple real-world examples of companies they know. For instance, if they love a particular toy or game company, explain how investing in that company means they have a part in its success.

4. Introducing Savings Jars:

   Extend the concept of saving to investing. Use a "Investing Jar" alongside their savings jar to demonstrate setting aside money for long-term goals. This visual representation helps them connect saving with the idea of investing.

5. Discussing Risk and Reward:

   Explain the concept of risk and reward in simple terms. Compare it to a game where sometimes you win, and sometimes you might not. This introduces the idea that investing involves a level of uncertainty.

6. Introducing Investment Accounts:

Discuss the idea of investment accounts. Explain that there are special places, like a "bank for investing," where their money can grow. This introduces the concept of financial institutions that facilitate investments.

7. Relating to Future Goals:

   Connect investing to future goals. Discuss how investing can help them achieve bigger things in the future, like buying a car, going to college, or even starting their own business.

8. Investing as a Team Effort:

   Frame investing as a team effort. Discuss how many people invest together to make things happen, similar to teamwork in sports or group activities.

9. Exploring Different Types of Investments:

Introduce the idea that there are different ways to invest. Discuss stocks as a way to own part of a company and bonds as a way to lend money to a company. Use simple language and examples to illustrate these concepts.

10. Learning from Mistakes:

Discuss the possibility of mistakes and losses in investing. Use age-appropriate examples to convey that sometimes things don't go as planned, but it's essential to learn from those experiences.

11. Regularly Checking Progress:

Emphasize the importance of checking on their investments regularly. This could be a simple monthly review to see how their "investment jar" is growing, reinforcing the idea of tracking progress.

12. Encourage Questions:

Foster a curious mindset by encouraging kids to ask questions about investing. Create an open environment where they feel comfortable exploring and understanding more about the world of investing.

By incorporating these simple concepts, parents and educators can provide a foundation for kids to grasp the basics of investing and instill a positive attitude towards long-term financial planning.

- **Exploring Investment Options for Kids**

While children may not engage in traditional investment options like adults, there are educational and practical ways to introduce them to the concept. Here are some avenues to explore:

1. Educational Apps and Games:
There are several apps and online games designed to teach kids about investing and money management. These platforms often simulate investment scenarios in a

kid-friendly manner, making the learning process interactive and engaging.

3. Savings Accounts:

While not a traditional investment, a savings account can serve as an introductory step. Many banks offer savings accounts for minors, providing a safe place for kids to store money and learn about the concept of earning interest.

4. Stocks:

  Introduce the idea of owning a small piece of a company by discussing stocks. Consider purchasing a few shares of a well-known company that the child is interested in. Use this as a tangible example to explain how the value of stocks can fluctuate.

5. Bonds:

  Simplify the concept of bonds by explaining them as a way to lend

money to a company or government.
Discuss how bonds work and
emphasize the concept of earning
interest over time.

6. Educational Investment Programs:
   Some financial institutions offer
educational programs designed for
young investors. These programs
often provide learning materials,
investment simulations, and guidance
to help kids understand the basics
of investing.

7. Mock Investment Portfolios:

Create a mock investment portfolio for educational purposes. Discuss hypothetical investments, track their performance, and explain how different factors can influence the value of these investments. This hands-on approach can make the learning experience more practical.

8. Discuss Real-World Investment Stories:

Share simple and relatable
investment success stories with
children. This could be stories about
companies they know or examples of
successful entrepreneurs.
Connecting investments to
real-world achievements can inspire
interest.

9. Explore Investment Books for
Kids:

There are educational books
tailored for children that explain

the basics of money, saving, and investing. Reading these books together can be an enjoyable way to introduce financial concepts.

10. Participate in Stock Market Simulations:

Engage in stock market simulations or games that allow kids to virtually invest in stocks. This provides a risk-free environment for them to practice making investment

decisions and understand market
dynamics.

11. Precious Metals:

   Introduce the concept of
investing in precious metals like gold
or silver. While physical ownership
might not be practical, discussing
the idea of these commodities as
investments can broaden their
understanding.

12. Explore Investment Clubs:

Some communities or schools have investment clubs or financial literacy programs for kids. Joining such clubs can provide an interactive and social learning environment.

It's crucial to adapt the complexity of investment discussions based on the child's age and comprehension level. The primary goal is to instill a basic understanding of financial principles and a positive attitude towards

responsible money management.

CHAPTER 6

Giving Back

- **The Importance of Philanthropy**

Teaching kids about the importance of philanthropy can foster empathy, compassion, and a sense of responsibility towards making a positive impact on the world. Here are strategies to impart

this valuable lesson:

1. Lead by Example:

   Demonstrate philanthropic

behavior by engaging in charitable

activities yourself. Whether it's

volunteering time, donating to a

cause, or participating in community

service, children often learn by

observing their role models.

2. Discuss Empathy:

Explain the concept of empathy and help children understand the feelings and needs of others. Share stories or examples that evoke empathy and compassion, emphasizing the idea that not everyone has the same privileges or resources.

3. Choose Age-Appropriate Causes: Select causes or charities that resonate with the child's interests or concerns. Whether it's helping

animals, supporting education, or
aiding those in need, aligning with
their passions makes philanthropy
more meaningful.

4. Involve Them in Decision-Making:
Include children in decisions
related to charitable giving. Discuss
various causes, show them different
charitable organizations, and let
them have a say in where donations
or volunteer efforts are directed.

5. Engage in Family Philanthropy Projects:

Initiate family philanthropy projects. This could be organizing a charity event, participating in a community clean-up, or collaborating on a project to help those in need. These shared experiences strengthen the family bond while instilling philanthropic values.

6. Use Everyday Opportunities:

Seize everyday situations to discuss philanthropy. Whether it's helping a neighbor, sharing with others, or expressing kindness, highlight the small acts that contribute to the well-being of the community.

7. Read Books on Philanthropy:
   Explore children's books that focus on kindness, giving, and making a positive impact. Reading stories with philanthropic themes can spark

conversations and help children relate to the importance of helping others.

8. Create a Philanthropy Jar:

Establish a "Philanthropy Jar" where family members contribute spare change or small amounts of money regularly. Discuss how this money will be used to support a cause, teaching kids that even modest contributions can make a difference.

9. Discuss Global Issues:

Depending on the child's age, introduce them to global issues in an age-appropriate manner. Discuss challenges faced by people around the world and brainstorm ways to contribute positively to addressing these issues.

10. Highlight Role Models:

Share stories of philanthropic individuals, both historical figures

and contemporary role models.
Discuss how their actions have made
a positive impact on society,
inspiring children to see the
potential for positive change.

11. Visit Charitable Organizations:
Arrange visits to local charitable
organizations or volunteer
opportunities. Seeing the work
firsthand can help children connect
with the impact of philanthropy and

understand the tangible results of their efforts.

12. Encourage Volunteering:

Actively involve children in volunteer activities. This hands-on experience provides a direct understanding of how their time and efforts contribute to the well-being of others.

By incorporating these strategies, parents and educators can instill in children a sense of social

responsibility and the understanding

that even small actions can

contribute to building a more

compassionate and caring world.

CHAPTER 7

Money and Technology

- **Digital Money and Online Transactions**

Teaching kids about digital money and online transactions is essential in today's technologically advanced world. Here are strategies to help children understand these concepts responsibly:

1. Explain Digital Currency:

Introduce the concept of digital currency by explaining that money can exist in digital form, not just as physical coins and bills. Discuss how people use digital money for various transactions.

2. Discuss Online Banking:

If applicable, show children how online banking works. Explain how people can manage their money, check balances, and transfer funds using computers or mobile devices.

3. Explore Digital Wallets:
Introduce the idea of digital wallets that store digital versions of credit cards, debit cards, or other payment methods. Discuss how these wallets can be used for online purchases.

4. Set Up a Virtual Allowance:

If children receive an allowance, consider setting up a virtual allowance system. Use an app or an online tool that allows them to track their allowance, savings, and spending digitally.

5. Teach Online Safety:

Emphasize the importance of online safety and security. Discuss the need for strong passwords,

avoiding sharing personal
information online, and being
cautious when using digital
platforms.

6. Explain Online Transactions:
   Walk through the process of
online transactions, from selecting
items to making a purchase. Discuss
the steps involved in entering
payment information and the
importance of confirming details
before completing a transaction.

7. Use Educational Apps:

Explore educational apps designed to teach kids about money and online transactions. These apps often gamify the learning process, making it engaging and interactive.

8. Discuss Different Payment Methods:

Explain various digital payment methods such as credit cards, debit cards, mobile payment apps, and online payment platforms. Discuss the differences between them and when each might be used.

9. Create a "Digital Money" Chart: Develop a visual chart or diagram illustrating the flow of digital money. Include earning, spending, saving, and investing aspects. This visual aid can help reinforce the understanding of digital financial processes.

10. Practice Making Transactions:

Engage in role-playing activities where children practice making online transactions. This could be through a simulated online store or by setting up scenarios that require digital payments.

11. Discuss the Benefits:

Talk about the advantages of using digital money, such as convenience, speed, and the ability to manage finances remotely.

Discuss how technology has evolved

to make financial transactions more

accessible.

12. Set Spending Limits:

   If children have access to digital

money, set spending limits and

discuss responsible spending habits.

This helps instill the concept of

budgeting even in the digital realm.

13. Discuss Digital Currency Risks:

Address the risks associated with digital currency, such as online fraud and scams. Teach kids to be vigilant and report any suspicious activity. Emphasize the importance of seeking guidance from trusted adults.

14. Review Digital Statements Together:

If applicable, regularly review digital statements together. Discuss transactions, monitor balances, and use these moments as opportunities to reinforce financial responsibility.

By incorporating these strategies, parents and educators can equip children with the knowledge and skills needed to navigate the digital financial landscape responsibly.

- **Teaching Responsible Tech Use in Finances**

Teaching kids responsible tech use in finances involves instilling good digital habits and promoting a healthy relationship with technology. Here are strategies to guide children in using technology responsibly for financial matters:

1. Explain Security Measures:
   Emphasize the importance of password security and the need to keep personal and financial

information private. Teach kids how to create strong, unique passwords and the significance of not sharing them.

2. Introduce Two-Factor Authentication:

Explain the concept of two-factor authentication and encourage its use whenever possible. This adds an extra layer of security to their online accounts, enhancing protection against unauthorized

access.

3. Teach Safe Online Practices:

Discuss safe online practices,

including recognizing and avoiding

phishing scams. Teach kids to verify

the legitimacy of websites and

emails before providing any financial

information.

4. Discuss the Consequences of

Oversharing:

Highlight the risks of oversharing on social media and other online platforms. Discuss how sharing too much personal information can compromise privacy and security.

5. Monitor App Permissions:
Show kids how to review and manage app permissions on their devices. Explain that granting unnecessary permissions can pose security risks, and they should only

allow access when it's essential for the app's functionality.

6. Encourage Regular Updates:

Stress the importance of keeping software, apps, and devices up to date. Updates often include security patches that help protect against vulnerabilities.

7. Set Time Limits:

Establish reasonable time limits for tech use, including financial apps and online platforms. Encourage a healthy balance between online and offline activities to prevent overreliance on screens.

8. Explain Digital Footprint:

Discuss the concept of a digital footprint and how online activities can leave a lasting impression. Teach kids to be mindful of what they post and share, as it can affect their reputation and future opportunities.

9. Use Parental Controls:

   Implement age-appropriate parental controls on devices and apps. These controls can help manage screen time, restrict access to certain content, and provide an additional layer of protection.

10. Discuss In-App Purchases:

   If kids have access to apps with in-app purchases, discuss the concept of spending real money within these apps. Set clear guidelines on when and how they can make purchases, emphasizing responsible decision-making.

11. Introduce Budgeting Apps:
   Explore age-appropriate budgeting apps designed for kids. These apps can make learning about money management engaging and interactive while providing a safe environment for financial exploration.

12. Model Responsible Tech Use:

Demonstrate responsible tech use through your own behavior. Children often mimic the habits of their parents or guardians, so modeling good practices sets a positive example.

13. Discuss Digital Responsibility:

Talk about the broader concept of digital responsibility, including how their online actions impact themselves and others. Encourage empathy and consideration for

others in their digital interactions.

14. Encourage Open Communication:

Establish an open line of

communication regarding tech use.

Encourage kids to share any

concerns or questions they may have

about online activities, fostering a

trusting relationship.

By incorporating these strategies,

parents and educators can guide

children in using technology
responsibly for financial activities
and promote a healthy and secure
digital experience.

CHAPTER 8

Parental Guidance and Support

- **Parental Role in Financial Education**

The parental role in financial education is crucial for equipping children with essential money management skills. Here are key aspects of the parental role in fostering financial literacy:

1. Lead by Example:

Parents serve as powerful role models. Demonstrating responsible financial habits, budgeting, and saving reinforces positive behaviors that children are likely to emulate.

2. Start Early:

Introduce financial concepts at an early age. Basic lessons about saving, spending, and the value of money can be incorporated into everyday activities.

3. Provide an Allowance:

Giving children an allowance can be a practical way to teach budgeting. It allows them to manage their money, make choices, and learn about the consequences of their spending decisions.

4. Encourage Saving:

Promote the habit of saving. Help children set savings goals and open a savings account. This instills the importance of delayed gratification and long-term financial planning.

5. Involve Children in Family Finances:

While maintaining age-appropriate boundaries, involve children in discussions about family finances.

This can include explaining budgeting decisions, planning for expenses, and discussing financial goals.

6. Teach Wise Spending:

Guide children in making wise spending choices. Discuss needs versus wants and encourage thoughtful decision-making when it comes to purchases.

7. Discuss Earning Money:

Encourage a strong work ethic by discussing the concept of earning money. Connect chores or responsibilities with the idea of compensation, teaching children that money is earned through effort.

8. Introduce Banking Concepts:
Teach children about banking, including the purpose of banks, how to deposit and withdraw money, and the concept of interest. Opening a

savings account for them can be a practical step.

9. Explore Financial Education Resources:

   Utilize age-appropriate financial education resources. There are books, games, and online tools designed to teach kids about money management in an engaging and accessible way.

10. Set Financial Goals Together:

Establish financial goals as a family. Whether it's saving for a vacation, a special purchase, or an educational fund, involve children in the goal-setting process.

11. Discuss Philanthropy and Giving Back:

Introduce the concept of philanthropy and charitable giving. Discuss the importance of contributing to the community and helping those in need.

12. Teach About Credit and Debt:

As children grow older, introduce concepts of credit and debt. Discuss responsible credit use and the potential consequences of accumulating debt.

13. Encourage Entrepreneurial Thinking:

Foster an entrepreneurial mindset. Encourage creativity, initiative, and problem-solving. This can involve simple ventures like a lemonade stand or more elaborate entrepreneurial endeavors as they grow older.

14. Promote Financial Independence: Gradually encourage financial independence as children mature. This includes guiding them in managing more aspects of their finances, such as budgeting for school expenses or part-time job earnings.

15. Maintain Open Communication:

Keep communication channels

open. Encourage children to ask

questions about money and financial

matters. Establishing an open

dialogue helps address concerns and

provides ongoing guidance.

By actively engaging in these

practices, parents play a pivotal role

in shaping their children's financial

attitudes and behaviors. Instilling

financial literacy from an early age
equips children with the skills they
need for a secure and responsible
financial future.

LAST WORDS FROM THE AUTHOR

As I conclude this exploration into the realm of financial education for young minds, I am filled with optimism for the future. Teaching kids about money is not just a task; it's a responsibility we bear collectively. In the pages of this book, we've delved into smart money moves, fostering habits that will serve as lifelong companions on the journey to financial well-being.

Remember, the seeds we plant today in the fertile soil of young minds will blossom into a landscape of empowered individuals tomorrow. Encourage curiosity, instill discipline, and foster a healthy relationship with money. Our children are not just the beneficiaries of our wisdom; they are the architects of a prosperous future.

May these lessons resonate beyond the pages and echo in conversations, classrooms, and homes. Let us stand united in the mission to equip the next generation with the financial acumen they need to thrive. Here's to a world where every child is not just financially aware but financially empowered.